First World War
and Army of Occupation
War Diary
France, Belgium and Germany

5 CAVALRY DIVISION
Divisional Troops
9 Light Armoured Battery
1 January 1917 - 30 October 1917

WO95/1163/2

The Naval & Military Press Ltd
www.nmarchive.com
Published in association with The National Archives

Published by

The Naval & Military Press Ltd

Unit 10 Ridgewood Industrial Park,

Uckfield, East Sussex,

TN22 5QE England

Tel: +44 (0) 1825 749494

www.naval-military-press.com

www.nmarchive.com

This diary has been reprinted in facsimile from the original. Any imperfections are inevitably reproduced and the quality may fall short of modern type and cartographic standards.

© **Crown Copyright**
Images reproduced by permission of The National Archives, London, England, 2015.

Contents

Document type	Place/Title	Date From	Date To
Heading	WO95/1163/2		
Heading	5th Cav Div 9th Light Armoured Battery. M.M. Gun S. 1917 Jan-Oct 1917		
Heading	War Diary of No. 9 Light Armoured Car Battery M.M.G.S From 1st January 1917 To 31st January 1917		
War Diary	Embreville	01/01/1917	21/03/1917
War Diary	Pont-De-Metz	22/03/1917	23/03/1917
War Diary	Estrees	24/03/1917	29/03/1917
War Diary	Peronne	30/03/1917	31/03/1917
War Diary	Villers-Bretonneux	01/04/1917	25/04/1917
War Diary	Guizencourt	26/04/1917	31/05/1917
War Diary	Tertry	01/06/1917	16/07/1917
War Diary	St. Pol	17/07/1917	04/08/1917
War Diary	Heuchin	05/08/1917	30/10/1917

WO 95/1163/2

~~2ND INDIAN CAVALRY DIVISION.~~

5th CAV DIV

9TH LIGHT ARMOURED BATTERY.

M.M. GUNS.

1917 JAN
~~JULY 1916~~ – OCT 1917.

FROM 2 INDIAN DIV TROOPS
Box 1182

B.E.F.

5 CAV DIV

NO BOX

SERIAL NO. 320.

Confidential

War Diary

of

No.9 LIGHT ARMOURED CAR BATTERY, M.M.G.S.

FROM 1st January 1917 TO 31st January 1917.

Army Form C. 2118.

WAR DIARY
or
INTELLIGENCE SUMMARY.
(Erase heading not required.)

Vol VII

9TH LIGHT ARMOURED BATTERY
M. M. G. S.

Place	Date	Hour	Summary of Events and Information	Remarks and references to Appendices
EMBREVILLE	Jan 1		Battery Training	
	2		"	
	3		"	
	4		m/115 645 Dvr Twehie from Base Depôt	
	5		" 1 Armoured Car proceeded to Cav Corps Head Quarters	
	6		"	
	7		"	
	8		" Capt Ronan proceeded to England. Dvr Kingsborough proceeded on leave to England	
	9		" 1 Armoured Car detail order to Cav Corps H.Q. Dvr Anderson from Hospital	
	10		"	
	11		"	
	12		"	
	13		"	
	14		" 22686 A/S Sm Kay R.a. transferred to 117th Jenny By 18th T.A.B 5th Army	
	15		" 22215 Gnr Anderson to Hospital. 3 Ton Lorry transferred to O.C Workshops	
	16		"	

Army Form C. 2118.

WAR DIARY
or
INTELLIGENCE SUMMARY.
(Erase heading not required.)

Place	Date	Hour	Summary of Events and Information	Remarks and references to Appendices
			9TH LIGHT ARMOURED BATTERY **M. M. G. S.**	
	17		Battery Training	
	18		" — Inspection of Bty by Corps Commander at "Auli".	
	19		"	
	20		"	
	21		"	
	22		" — D.R.O. Dpers received on leave to England	
	23		"	
	24		"	
	25		" — M/020817 Pte Kingsborough from leave to England.	
	26		"	
	27		"	
	28		"	
	29		"	
	30		"	
	31		"	

J. Buckham Lt.
COMDG. 9TH LIGHT ARMOURED BATTERY,
M. M. G. S.

Army Form C. 2118.

WAR DIARY
or
INTELLIGENCE SUMMARY.
(Erase heading not required.)

Vol VIII
9th L.A.A. Bty

Place	Date	Hour	Summary of Events and Information	Remarks and references to Appendices
EMBREVILLE	17		Battery training R to Lyne to R.A. Base Depot.	
	18		Capt Ronan reported from Hospital "ROUEN".	
	19		"	
	20		Armoured Car M231 with two trucks a new Self starter to "St Omer" Havre self starter fitted.	
	21		Cpl Sawyer returned from Rdtr. signalling course.	
	22		"	
	23		Armoured Car M230 with driver Cpl Stephens to Ordnance Workshop "CALAIS"	
	24		"	
	25		"	
	26		"	
	27		"	
	28		"	

T. Ronan Capt.
COMDG. 9TH L.A.A. BATTERY.

Army Form C. 2118.

WAR DIARY
or
INTELLIGENCE SUMMARY.
(Erase heading not required.)

Instructions regarding War Diaries and Intelligence Summaries are contained in F. S. Regs., Part II. and the Staff Manual respectively. Title pages will be prepared in manuscript.

Place	Date	Hour	Summary of Events and Information	Remarks and references to Appendices
EMBREVILLE	17		Battery Journey of R.C Lyns to R.A Base Depot.	
	18	"	Capt Ronan reported from Hospital "Rouen"	
	19	"	"	
	20	"	Arrived from M.231 with two turpaulins Lapl Powers to St Omer HQrs	
	21	"	aerly starter fixed	
	22	"	Cpl Sawyer returned from R.R.G Reporting Comm	
	23	"	Arrived Cars M.123 and M.126 Cpl Stephens to Ordnance Workshop Calais	
	24	"	"	
	25	"	"	
	26	"	"	
	27	"	"	
	28	"	"	

J. Ronan Capt.
COMDG. 8TH LIGHT ARMOURED BATTERY, M.M.G.S.

Army Form C. 2118.

WAR DIARY
or
INTELLIGENCE SUMMARY.
(Erase heading not required.)

Vol IX

Instructions regarding War Diaries and Intelligence Summaries are contained in F. S. Regs., Part II. and the Staff Manual respectively. Title pages will be prepared in manuscript.

9TH LIGHT ARMOURED BATTERY
M. M. G. S.

Place	Date	Hour	Summary of Events and Information	Remarks and references to Appendices
	Mch			
KANTREVILLE	1		Battery training	
	2		(2) Armoured Cars with 3rd Infantry to Belgian Range for firing practice	
	3		Battery training	
	4		"	
	5		(2) Armoured Cars with 3rd Infantry to Belgian Range for firing practice	
	6		Firing practice on Reconnoitered Range with Vickers Maxim rifles	
	7		"	
	8		"	
	9		Battery training	
	10		"	
	11		" 3rd Infantry to Belgian Range for firing practice	
	12		"	
	13		"	
	14		" 2/Lt Burnham Osborne with R.E. Dept for aeroplane training	
	15		"	
	16		"	

Army Form C. 2118.

WAR DIARY
or
INTELLIGENCE SUMMARY.
(Erase heading not required.)

Instructions regarding War Diaries and Intelligence Summaries are contained in F.S. Regs., Part II. and the Staff Manual respectively. Title pages will be prepared in manuscript.

Summary of Events and Information

9TH LIGHT ARMOURED BATTERY
M.M.G.S.

Place	Date	Hour	Summary of Events and Information	Remarks and references to Appendices
EMBREVILLE	Mch. 17		Battery training	
	18		"	
	19		Inspection by Lt. Col. Bradney, Car Corps, M.G. Officer	
	20		Battery training	
	21		Battery moved from EMBREVILLE to PONT-DE-METZ	
PONT-DE-METZ	22		Battery stood by " "	
	23		" moved from PONT-DE-METZ to ESTREES	
ESTREES	24		" stood by	
	25		(H) Armoured Cars proceeded on Reconnaissance	
	26		(2) " " in action	
	27		(2) " " OC ammunitionated Emr Bernard severely wounded	
	28		Battery stood by Emr Bernard not withstanding moved from observing station to PERONNE	
	29		" moved from ESTREES to PERONNE 2pm	
	30		" stood by Emr Bernard buried. Battery moved from PERONNE to VILLERS-BRETONNEUX	
PERONNE	31		Battery training	

W.E.W. Fromany
COMDG. 9th LIGHT ARMOURED BATTERY,
M.M.G.S.

Army Form C. 2118.

Vol 10

WAR DIARY
or
INTELLIGENCE SUMMARY.
(Erase heading not required.)

Summary of Events and Information

"LIGHT ARMOURED BATTERY"
M. M. G. S.

Place	Date	Hour		Remarks and references to Appendices
VILLERS-	Apl 1		Battery training	
BRETONNEUX	2		"	
	3		"	
	4		"	
	5		"	
	6		4 Armoured Cars with 28 O.R men & Lt Nightman & Osborne to 3rd A.N.S repair shop	
	7		Armoured Cars to Australians for Allenson repairs	
	8			
	9		2 Nightman Gone to England	
	10		VILLERS-BRETONNEUX	
	11		7.30 am 3 Officers Reconnaissance run to	
	12			
	13		GIZENCOURT	
	14		"16 car Rob, who kept Lorry, under Lt Henderson to Lt Henderson	
BRETONNEUX	15		2 Armoured Cars with Lt Winters - Bretonneux	
	16		proceeded to GUZENCOURT	

Army Form C. 2118.

WAR DIARY
or
INTELLIGENCE SUMMARY.
(Erase heading not required.)

Instructions regarding War Diaries and Intelligence Summaries are contained in F. S. Regs., Part II. and the Staff Manual respectively. Title pages will be prepared in manuscript.

8th LIGHT ARMOURED BATTERY
M. M. G. S.

Place	Date	Hour	Summary of Events and Information	Remarks and references to Appendices
	Apl 2			
	17		Armoured Cars to repair workshops at 3rd A.R.C. repair shops	
	18		"	
	19		"	
	20		"	
	21		"	
	22		"	
	23		" Lieutenant Rose home to England	
	24		" Villers - Bretonneux	
	25		" 8 L.C.B. to Guizencourt	
			Remainder de—	
GUIZENCOURT	26		2 Armoured Cars from 2nd A.R.S. repair shops. 2 Armoured Cars for armament work	
	27		Battery Training	
	28		"	
	29		"	
	30		"	

M. Wrightman
O.C. 8 Lt. Armoured Battery
M. M. G. S.

T2134. Wt. W708—776. 500000. 4/15. Sir J. C. & S.

Army Form C. 2118.

Andale Bty
Vol XI

WAR DIARY
or
INTELLIGENCE SUMMARY.
(Erase heading not required.)

Summary of Events and Information

9TH LIGHT ARMOURED BATTERY M. M. G. S.

Place	Date	Hour	Summary of Events and Information	Remarks and references to Appendices
GUIZENCOURT	MAY 1		Battery Training	
	2		"	
	3		"	
	4		"	
	5		"	
	6		"	
	7		"	
	8		"	
	9		"	
	10		"	
	11		"	
	12		"	
	13		"	
	14	2 p.m.	2 Lorries, 11 dondas, and 20 NCO's men under Lt Henderson to "TERTRY" 4 Armoured Cars & 1 Tender lorry with 26 NCO's men under Lt W.E. Wightman & Lt G.A. Osborne to "BIHECOURT"	JBuckum Lt for
	15		Battery standing by	
	16		"	

Army Form C. 2118.

WAR DIARY
or
INTELLIGENCE SUMMARY.
(Erase heading not required.)

Instructions regarding War Diaries and Intelligence Summaries are contained in F. S. Regs., Part II. and the Staff Manual respectively. Title pages will be prepared in manuscript.

8TH LIGHT ARMOURED BATTERY M. M. G. S.

Place	Date	Hour	Summary of Events and Information	Remarks and references to Appendices
	MAY			
	17		Battery standing by.	
	18		" " "	
	19		" " "	
	20		8 N.C.O'men with 2 Vickers M.G's under Lt. G.H. Osborne to advanced posts.	
	21		Battery standing by.	
	22		8 N.C.O'men with 2 Vickers M.G's under Lt. G.H. Osborne relieved from advanced posts	
	23		Battery standing by	
	24		8 N.C.O'men with 2 Vickers M.G's under Lt. G.H. Osborne to main trench	
	25		Battery standing by	
	26		" " "	
	27		" " "	
	28		8 N.C.O'men with 2 Vickers M.G's under Lt. G.H. Osborne relieved from main trench	
	29		Battery standing by. 2/Lt. McMillan with crew to "BIHECOURT"	
	30		" " "	
	31		" " "	

Army Form C. 2118.

WAR DIARY
or
INTELLIGENCE SUMMARY.
(Erase heading not required.)

Summary of Events and Information
9TH LIGHT ARMOURED BATTERY
M. M. G. S.

Place	Date	Hour	Summary of Events and Information	Remarks and references to Appendices
TERTRY	June 1		Battery standing by	Quarterly return Gunners & M Gunners 30-6-17
	2			
	3		23 O.Rs from 1st L.A.B. assumed command	
	4		2nd Lt. Mannus R.D. evacuated to 39 C.C.S. wounded in gas attack	
	5			
	6			
	7		2 M.G's removed to posn S.E. of St QUENTIN. Low B-HECOURT	
	8			
	9			
	10			
	11			
	12			
	13			
	14			
	15			
	16		6914 Pte McKinlay from M.G.C. Base Depot	
	17			
	18			
	19			
	20			
	21			
	22			

COMDG. 9TH L.A. M.M.G.S. BATTERY

WAR DIARY
or
INTELLIGENCE SUMMARY.
(Erase heading not required.)

9TH LIGHT ARMOURED BATTERY
Summary of Events and Information
M. M. G. S.

Army Form C. 2118.

Place	Date June	Hour	Remarks and references to Appendices
VERTRY	23		Battery observing Bn 2.M.G. reinforcement from 2nd, 3rd & 5th Squadron to Bricourt.
	24		OC proceeded to A.1.6 reserve Depot St Omer.
	25		
	26		OC returned from A.1.6 reserve Depot St Omer.
	27		2 M.G. received on loan in charge of OC 4th M.G. Squadron (returned by squadron)
	28		8x Body 24 (8) march 14, 1st Sen Harris, Sgt Simon, 2 Sgt moved to A.1.6 reserve Depot St Omer.
	29		8x Body 2 let out 20 Ky Megahan Sgt Stevens, Lou Moranel four Ascoyeux shipped St Omer. 3 M.G. received under 10 K Moland to Tincourt for scale & serving Sale.
	30		Lt. H. Bentham returned to G.H. Osborne at Tincourt.

COMDG. 9TH L.A. BATTERY,
M. M. G. S.

Army Form C. 2118.

WAR DIARY
or
INTELLIGENCE SUMMARY.
(Erase heading not required.)

Summary of Events and Information

9TH LIGHT ARMOURED BATTERY
M. M. G. S.

Place	Date	Hour	Summary of Events and Information	Remarks and references to Appendices
TERTRY	July 1		Battery Training	
	2		" "	
	3		" "	
	4		" "	
	5		" "	
	6		" "	
	7		" "	
	8		" "	
	9		" "	
	10		" "	
	11		" "	
	12		" "	
	13		" "	
	14		" "	
	15		" "	
	16	8am	Battery transferred from "TERTRY" to "ST POx" arriving at 3.30 pm	
St. Pox	17		Battery Training. 2nd Lt Beacham proceeded on leave to U.K.	
	18		" " 4 Armoured Cars exchanged with 7th L.A.M. By.	

Sgd [signature]
COMDG. 9TH LIGHT ARMOURED BATTERY,
M. M. G. S.

WAR DIARY
or
INTELLIGENCE SUMMARY.
(Erase heading not required.)

Army Form C. 2118.

9TH LIGHT ARMOURED BATTERY
M. M. G. S.

Place	Date	Hour	Summary of Events and Information	Remarks and references to Appendices
	July 19		Battery Training. M2/147907 Pte Bircham proceeded on leave to U.K.	
	20		"	
	21		"	
	22		D. C. A. Osborne proceeded on leave to UK	
	23		"	
	24	9.30 am	Battery proceeded to Ranges with Vickers M G for firing practice	
	25		Battery Training	
	26		"	
	27	9.30 am	Battery proceeded to Ranges with Vickers, tolerating rifles rifles for firing practice	
	28		Battery Training	
	29		" Lt A Bentham reported from leave to U.K.	
	30		" M2/147907 Pte Anderson returned from leave to U.K.	
	31	9.30 am	Battery proceeded to Ranges with Vickers M G for firing practice	

COMDG. 9TH LIGHT ARMOURED BATTERY,
M. M. G. S.

WAR DIARY
or
INTELLIGENCE SUMMARY.
(Erase heading not required.)

Army Form C. 2118.

Place	Date August	Hour	Summary of Events and Information	Remarks and references to Appendices
ST POL	1		Battery training	
	2		Lce/Cpl O'Too proceeded on leave to U.K.	
	3		32621 Pte G. Johnson proceeded leave to UK	
	4		Battery moved from St Pol to Heuchin	
HEUCHIN	5		Battery training. Lt N.E. Magretson rejoined from leave UK	
	6			
	7			
	8			
	9			
	10		2 Armoured Cars reported on the journey from Amiens BD	
	11		3.39pm Cpl Nicol proceeded on leave to Paris	
	12			
	13		Capt O'Too proc leave to UK	
	14		32577 Pte Leonstar proc leave to UK	
	15			
	16			
	17		Lt W.E. Wightmore proc leave to UK	
	18			
	19			
	20		CO proceeded to "Calais" re Armoured Cars M	
	21			
	22			

Army Form C. 2118.

WAR DIARY
or
INTELLIGENCE SUMMARY.
(Erase heading not required.)

Instructions regarding War Diaries and Intelligence Summaries are contained in F. S. Regs., Part II. and the Staff Manual respectively. Title pages will be prepared in manuscript.

Place	Date	Hour	Summary of Events and Information	Remarks and references to Appendices
HEUCHIN	23		Battery training	
	24		"	
	25		"	
	26		" 138856 Sgt Venion D. promoted sd. Sgt. (Authority P/6/6186.	
	27		" 1476 Gnr Reed J.E.) proceeded on leave to U.K.	
			" 736257 Gnr Yate)	
	28		"	
	29		" 2389 Gnr Cook proceeded on leave to U.K.	
	30		"	
	31		"	

O.J. [signature], Capt.
Comdg. 8th. [?] Cdn. Armoured Battery.

Serial No. 320

WAR DIARY
or
INTELLIGENCE SUMMARY.

9TH LIGHT ARMOURED BATTERY
M.M.G.S.

Army Form C. 2118.

(Erase heading not required.)

September 1914

Place	Date	Hour	Summary of Events and Information	Remarks and references to Appendices
Fenchin	1		Battery Training	
	2		" "	
	3		" "	
	4		" "	
	5		" "	
	6		" "	
	7		" "	
	8		" "	
	9		" "	
	10		" "	
	11		" "	
	12		" "	
	13		" "	
	14		" "	
	15		" "	
	16		" "	
	17		" "	
	18		" "	
	19		" "	
	20		" "	
	21		" "	
	22		" "	
	23		" "	
	24		" "	
	25		" "	
	26		" "	
	27		" "	
	28		" "	
	29		" "	
	30		" "	

J. Wiseman Capt.
COMDG. 9TH LIGHT ARMOURED BATTERY,
M.M.G.S.

WAR DIARY
or
INTELLIGENCE SUMMARY.
(Erase heading not required.)

Army Form C. 2118.

9TH LIGHT ARMOURED BATTERY
M. M. G. S.

Place	Date	Hour	Summary of Events and Information	Remarks and references to Appendices
Houchin	1-30		Battery Training	

[signature]
Capt.
COMDG. 9TH LIGHT ARMOURED BATTERY.
M. M. G. S.

www.ingramcontent.com/pod-product-compliance
Lightning Source LLC
Chambersburg PA
CBHW081252170426
43191CB00037B/2126